Abstract Colouring Book

Volume 2
Pattern Designs

by

June Krisko

jkc reative
publishing

Published by JK Creative Publishing in 2015
First edition; First printing

Illustrations and design © 2015 June Krisko

http://www.jkcreativepublishing.com

ISBN   978-0-9949584-1-9

I dedicate this book to Jerri and Frank for all their continued support.

I feel colour in my soul.

Strutting along in peacock green.

Lighting up the page with neon yellow.

Periwinkle twinkle time.

Having a siesta in Spanish orange.

Colouring my crown in imperial violet.

Lemon drops in my puddle.

Roasting in chestnut brown.

Being creative with indigo blue.

Falling for pumpkin orange.

Parrot green talks a lot.

Moss green is growing on my walkway.

Waking up with espresso.

True green is so honest.

Adding some cream to the page.

Working through the process red.

Embarrassed by blush pink.

Crunchy apple green.

Stuck on permanent red.

Seeing petals with poppy red.

Walking along sandbar brown.

Growing tall with grass green.

Spicy moments with mulberry.

Green ogre or green ochre?

Seashell pink found on the seashore.

Turning it down with muted turquoise.

Tickled by pink.

Flowery dahlia purple.

Travelling to Copenhagen blue.

Warmed by terra cotta.

Decorative style with henna.

Craving my chocolate.

Mysterious and dark purple.

Rocking it with mineral orange.

Underwater with kelp green.

Juicy black cherry.

Tapping into sap green light.

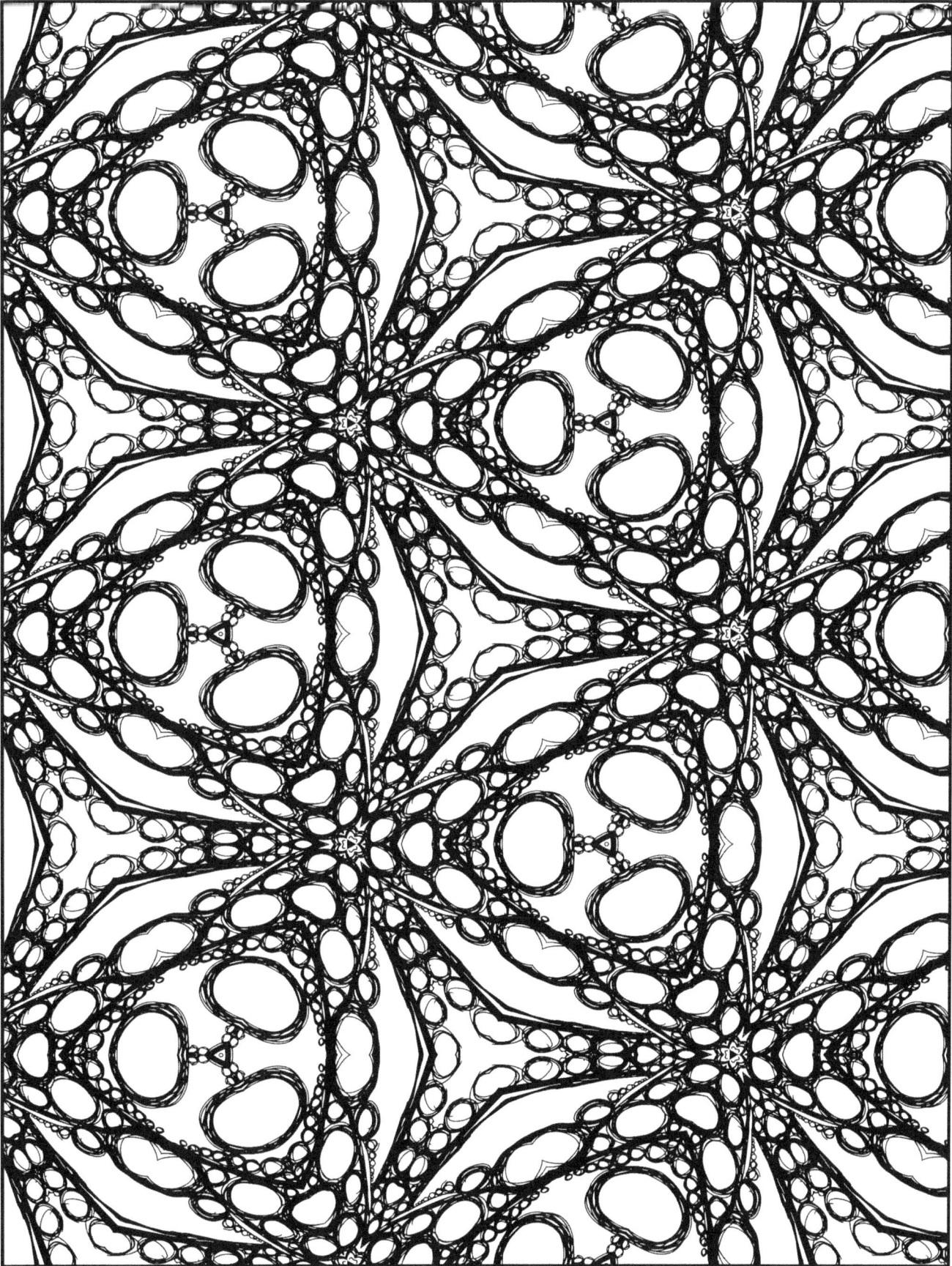

Brightened by sunburst yellow.

Fuzzy days with peach.

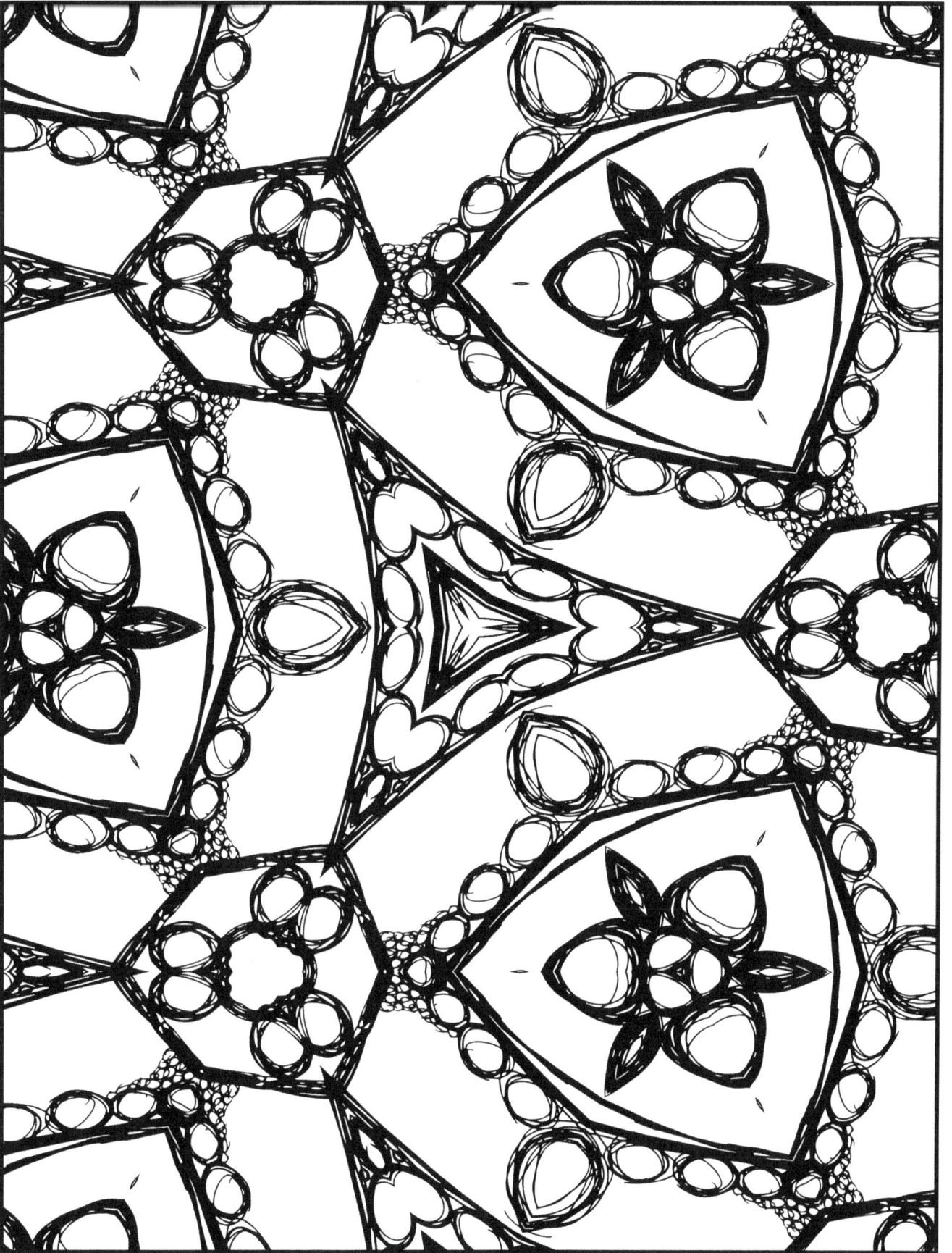

Drape the black grape.

Captured by salmon pink.

On fire with burnt ochre.

Lumber with dark umber.

Windy scarlett lake.

Pretty violet blue.

Jewels of ruby red.

Delicate china blue.

Feeling wired using electric blue.

Saluting my marine green.

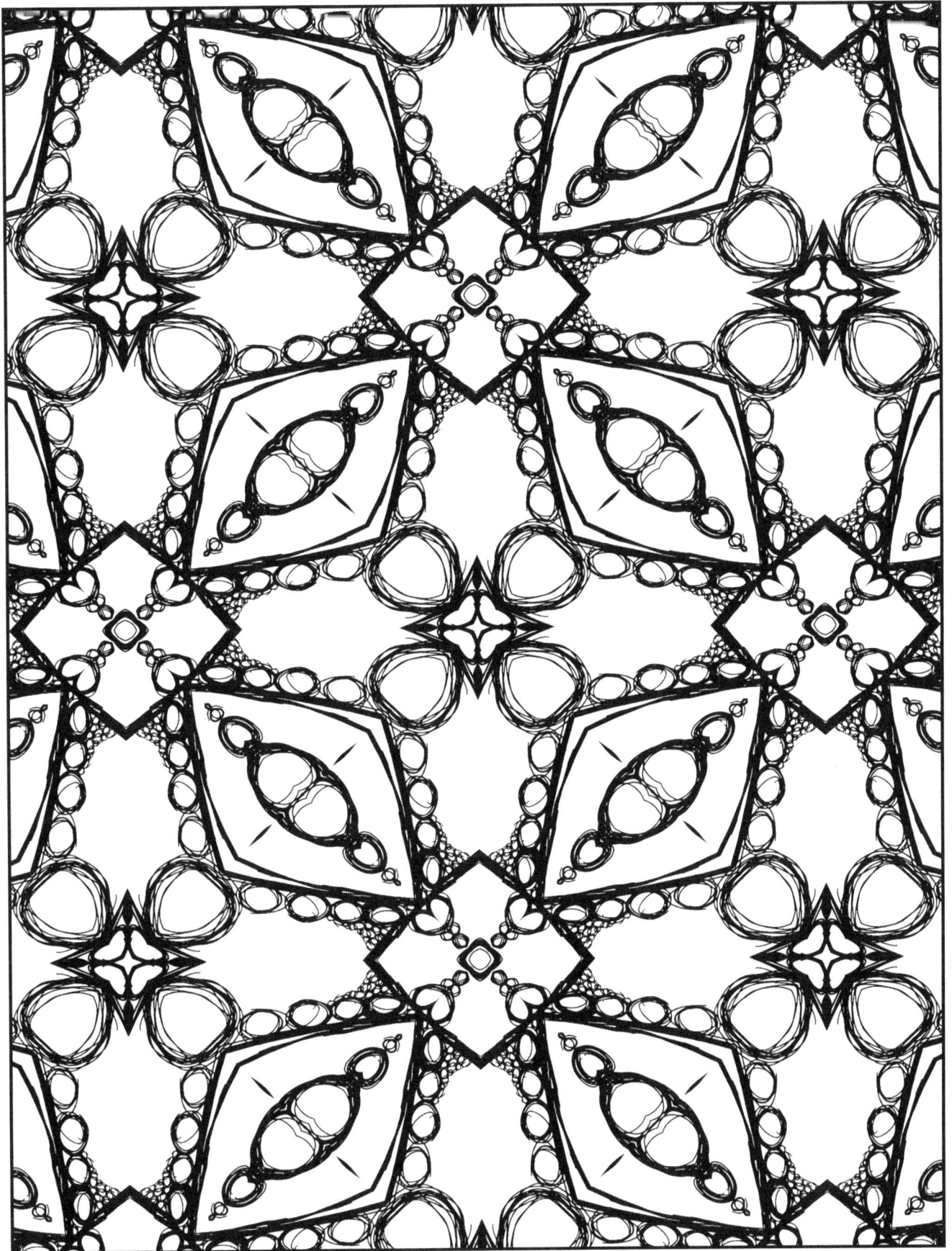

Coming soon...

Look for more
"Abstract Colouring Books"
and other types
of colouring books
online at
www.jkcreativepublishing.com.

June Krisko is a digital artist and
photographer.

Born and raised in Canada, she studied
Fine Arts at Redeemer College
and Crafts & Design at Sheridan College.

She uses various digital techniques
to create one-of-a-kind abstract works
of art for publication.